GROUND ZERO

GROUND ZERO

A COLLECTION OF CHICAGO POEMS

MARC KELLY SMITH

EDITED BY MARK ELEVELD
INTRODUCTION BY PATRICIA SMITH

TriQuarterly Books/Northwestern University Press
Evanston, Illinois

TriQuarterly Books
Northwestern University Press
www.nupress.northwestern.edu

Printed in the United States of America

10 9 8 7 6 5 4 3 2 1

Library of Congress Cataloging-in-Publication Data

Names: Smith, Marc Kelly, author. | Smith, Patricia, 1955– writer of added commentary.
Title: Ground zero : a collection of Chicago poems / Marc Kelly Smith.
Description: Evanston, Illinois : TriQuarterly Books/Northwestern University Press,
    2021.
Identifiers: LCCN 2020029547 | ISBN 9780810143081 (paperback) | ISBN
    9780810143098 (ebook)
Subjects: LCSH: Chicago (Ill.)—Poetry. | LCGFT: Poetry.
Classification: LCC PS3569.M537637 G76 2021 | DDC 811/.54—dc23
LC record available at https://lccn.loc.gov/2020029547

CONTENTS

EDITOR'S INTRODUCTION

This collection celebrates the poet and artist Marc Kelly Smith, who has presided over the most significant literary movement in Chicago in a generation. These are the poems he has performed around the world for over forty years. Who is Marc? He is Chicago. He is more Mike Royko than Studs Terkel, more Nelson Algren than Saul Bellow. What does that mean? That he is his own man. He is perfectly flawed. He is dangerous. The artist Tony Fitzpatrick observed that Marc is the most contrarian poet he's ever been around. Marc is the perennial outsider whose own creativity has made him one of the most famous and successful poets of his generation. And he did it his way. And as Patricia Smith, the greatest living poet, says in her wonderful statement about Marc, poetry slams, and Chicago, it had to be Marc. Marc founded the poetry slam. He came up with the idea. The show is his. The way the Uptown Poetry Slam was run was purposeful, with intent and philosophy. It was curated. It didn't become the longest-running show in Chicago by accident. It was Marc. At the Midland Authors Society Edward Hirsch leaned into Marc and said, "What you created is beautiful." And because Marc grew up by the steel mills on the South Side of the most segregated city in the country, his response to Edward was, "I know."

What sort of audacity allows such a reply? Imagine sitting on a stage every Sunday since 1988, listening to three hours of poems. Every week. Three hours. Imagine the love poems, the mother poems, the god-awful "me me me, my pain my pain my pain" poems. Imagine being moved by the quiet dental hygienist who reads her poem on stage for the first time. Marc was there for that. Imagine the size of the poet egos. For all those years. Marc was there for that. Imagine providing a stage for poets, working to craft an audience, and then the poet getting offstage and bad mouthing you. Or, the poet getting offstage and thanking Marc for one of the most moving experiences of their life. Imagine sitting onstage for a diverse Chicago audience through Bush, Clinton, Bush, Obama, Trump. Do you let the poet who you don't agree with read their poem? Does it piss off other poets? Or is the job to get as many voices as possible onstage and let the social experiment of democracy take over? Does Bukowski or Genet or Dybek or Sandberg get published in today's world? Standing next to a recent Pulitzer Prize winner who was confronted about the poetry slam founder Marc Smith, he said something to the effect that, it's his stage, if you don't like it, don't come. Does anyone realize how hard he's worked at this thing? When Marc went to see Robert Pinsky perform his wonderful PoemJazz session at the

Green Mill Jazz Lounge, Robert asked if this is where the poetry slam started. And Marc put up his hands and replied, I built this house. Like Michael Jordan raising the last trophy at the United Center. Marc Smith is a poet. This is his book of poems. Marc has left Chicago just like Algren and Bellow. I don't know if there will ever be another Uptown Poetry Slam in Chicago. Patricia Smith was there at the beginning. She is our greatest living poet. I have seen Patricia at the Green Mill screaming to Marc, "Do 'Ground Zero'! Perform 'Ground Zero'!" Her introduction gets the wildfire of commingling poetics perfectly. She understands. She gets it right: "No one—no one—could have done this but him."

Mark Eleveld

THE SECOND THROAT

Poetry Slam

Patricia Smith

In August 1999, the tenth-anniversary National Poetry Slam was held in Chicago. Depending on whom you talked to, the slam either strode back home sporting a cocky grin and a glittering, lopsided crown, or she limped in from a back alley, jittery and bruised, avoiding direct eye contact and reluctantly showing her age.

By the time the celebrated and vilified poetry competition reached double digits, everyone in the poetry community and many beyond it had an opinion. The slam was necessary breath, a rousing kick in the rear for an art form that wheezed dust and structure. Or it was a death knell for the genre, a brash and quirky theater complete with scorecards; unruly poetics by common, untenured folk; and "judges" who were actually prized for their lack of qualifications.

But no matter how you felt about her, the ole girl had certainly grown up. And everyone agreed that she couldn't have been born anywhere else.

My hometown is the land of blatant politicking, Vienna hot dogs at five in the morning, and the city as a mean but efficient machine. It's Mayor Daley (Richard, not Richie); nasty, gut-level blues guitar; and the sprawling specter of the housing project Cabrini-Green, the blackened windows of its abandoned units like missing teeth in an already-rotted smile. Chicago is cops with their guts spilling over their belts, the riots in '68, midwestern "howdy," and Big Apple envy. It is sly and beauteous and unbridled drumbeat. The slam, ragged and mesmerizing, had the gall to tweak language and rattle convention while serving drinks on the side. It was the Windy's, in and through.

The final of the four-day National Slam was held in the 3,600-seat Chicago Theater, that gaudy State Street showplace with the megawatt marquee grin—the letters C-H-I-C-A-G-O lined up vertically and twinkling relentlessly, reminding locals that it was still among the city's dwindling downtown entertainment options and providing tourists with the perfect wish-you-were-here backdrop for their cheery digital pix. Despite its inner opulence, the theater sat on the edge of a downtown that had given up on transformation. Buy a coat dripping mink at Marshall Field's and then walk half a block to get a flimsy paper plate heaped with oily, artery-cramming soul food. Ah, yes, the slam was back home.

The concluding night of nationals had come a long way from its lower wattage counterpart a decade before. This time, more than three thousand people packed the theater. A number of former competitors, having moved on to greater and more profitable glories, dotted the crowd like celebs on Oscar night. Morley Safer of *60 Minutes* was in attendance, and even he couldn't keep a little awe from seeping into his "I've been in war zones and nothing fazes me" countenance. Cameras from FOX and CNN scanned the chattering audience. For weeks, predictably, the local media had been saturated with stories "discovering" the slam. Again.

But beneath its tendency to glitter, the night had that prideful, pieced-together feel that typifies an ongoing revolution. Those who'd been involved from the beginning linked eyes and nodded imperceptibly, rueful little smiles playing at the corners of their mouths. A paper bag wrapped around a bottle of bargain red vino made its way stealthily down one of the theater's fancy aisles. Nervous competitors mumbled their lines like mantras, repeatedly, repeatedly, repeatedly. Downtown and uptown were both sitting in the fancy seats—and though no one was gearing up for an inspiring rendition of "The Impossible Dream," no punches had been thrown. But it was Chicago, and it was still early.

Darting about the theater, his eyes meaningfully manic, Marc Kelly Smith did what he's always done so masterfully—he dropped like fuel on a fire that, up until then, everyone thought had been contained. The ex-construction worker had passed up a lucrative job with the city (all Chicago construction workers eventually wind up working for the city, and in Chicago, if you work for the city—just sayin'—you can pretty much count on lucrative) and surrendered a steady paycheck, choosing instead to wallow in the heady come-on of a very small limelight. Anyone who knows Marc knows that if it hadn't been for the slam, he would have crafted another outlet that would've allowed him to be both ringleader and ringmaster, the lion tamer and the droopy-eyed clown. He'd need to conjure a safe haven for a heart that cracked all too often and easily, a rubber-walled room to store his rampaging ego when he wasn't using it, and a place—with a reliable mic, a jukebox, and snazzy lighting—where he could trade rhythmic war stories with other flawed, fallible, and occasionally narcissistic human beings.

Marc was just enough of all of us—a heartbroken souse, madly in love with lyric and leaving shards of his self-esteem on beer-slick floors. We appreciated his litany of failures and trusted him with our collective voice, trusted him to wail the stories we were afraid of. Punch-drunk, he took the falls for us and then scrambled to his feet, facing off the next flurry of fists. We lived vicariously through the sexy riveting mess of him. Behind the mic, he wore our fears proudly. The stifled halls of academia wouldn't have had a clue about how to handle him. His words flowed like barroom light through a crack in a wooden door; he needed fools like us to cheer him on, and we needed him to trumpet the syllables we wouldn't dare. No one—no one—could have done this but him. He would be vilified, underestimated, misunderstood, and attacked. He would be blamed for both his successes and his failures. His fiery poetics would be dismissed as mere snippets of theater, and the kingdom he had crafted would be pointed to as an example of what poetry can be if the unwashed, untrained, and underfunded get ahold of it.

No one else would have held on so tightly, crazed and committed enough to see the madness through to this inevitable moment of box-office respectability. At the tenth anniversary of the National Poetry Slam, the undisputed daddy of the chaos slapped backs, pumped hands, charmed the media, scanned his kingdom, and tried to keep his eyes from wandering upward to behold a chandelier the size of a small country, a sight that would have undoubtedly caused reality to overwhelm him. He would not have been able to keep from bellowing over everyone and everything, "We're in the fucking Chicago Theater!"

My only part in the proceedings that evening was a short opening performance with Marc, Cin Salach, and Dean Hacker, fellow members of the team who'd snatched all the marbles at the very first national championship a decade before in San Francisco. All those lifetimes ago, we stunned everyone who encountered us, busting the boundary between stage and audience, leaving the podium and joining listeners in their seats, providing them with no way at all to turn away from stanzas that simply didn't know their rightful place. We did what we'd been doing all along in Chicago while assuming that everyone else was doing it too. But we'd been existing in a feverish bubble and, as far as the rest of the poetry world was concerned, nothing like us ever was.

Ten years from that triumph, we hurriedly huddled and managed to pull together a brief collaborative piece highlighting each of our voices. Backstage was teeming with edgy competitors, dizzy with bloodlust, thinking of slam as head-to-head, line-by-line warfare. But the four of us were proof that there was life beyond the score sheets, that the words went deeper and friendships were forged.

I was under no illusion that the majority of the audience would know any of us except for Marc or understand why we were delaying the meatier part of the show with our feisty little wordplay. The slam had grown so huge so rapidly, and each year a little of the history—the faces and voices and almost embarrassing hunger of those who nurtured the beast in its early days—fell by the wayside and was later trampled by poets stampeding toward recording contracts, television commercials, and the bright lights of Broadway.

With each passing year, I admit feeling a palpable sense of loss and a growing disconnect as new faces and rituals flood the slam landscape. Standing there in the Chicago Theater all those years later, I wanted to tell everyone how fierce and boundless and sloppy those first days were; how I lived and died for that Sunday night at the Green Mill; how I ached for Marc's addicting, godlike approval and guidance; how desperately I craved audience; and how the rush of words frightened me, spilling from my body like an expulsion of fever. But increasingly, whenever I would corner some poetry ingénue and start babbling about the wonders of yesteryear, eager to sense that same fever in her, I was indulged with a glazed but respectful gaze, not unlike the one kids give elders who are not yet completely useless but not useful in the ways they once were.

Here's what I'd tell them if I could.

At the Green Mill, there were eight open slots every Sunday. Anyone could sign up. The judges were people picked at random from the audience. They could be English professors, unemployed welders, or high school students. They didn't have to know poetry. It was our job to introduce them to it. The judges would listen to the poets in turn and judge them on a scale from 1 to 10, the scores based on both the content and delivery of the poems. Judges were monsters or saints, depending on the poem, the crowd, the poet, Marc Smith's sly indicators of yea or nay, the strength of the drinks, the weather. The whole thing was a statistically catastrophic crapshoot, art on a dartboard. It was the most beautiful thing I had ever seen.

The Green Mill was a long room cloaked in a maroon darkness, a cavern peppered with the twinkle of neon. Imagine the battered bar, the comfortably gruff barkeep, the overwrought grand piano at the front of the room, and Patsy Cline unfurling silk in the jukebox. Throughout the years, I heard bits and pieces of the Mill's sweet mystery: The name? A tribute to France's Moulin Rouge (Red Mill) but *green* so as not to be linked to the city's numerous red-light districts. By 1910, the joint had morphed into the Green Mill Gardens, an outdoor dancing and drinking spot frequented by Sophie Tucker and Al Jolson.

But the stories didn't get juicy until Al Capone entered the mix. His head henchman, "Machine gun" Jack McGurn, obtained a 25 percent ownership of the club. As the story goes, he slit the throat and lopped off the tongue of comedian/singer Joe E. Lewis when the entertainer threatened to move his act to another club. The scene, and the Mill, were re-created in the film *The Joker Is Wild*, starring Frank Sinatra.

That's the true stuff. But I also I heard, over and over again, with no proof whatsoever, that Al Capone had blasted a piano player off his bench because a tune was not to his liking. I loved that story because it fit so perfectly with the spirit of the slam: entertain me, or your time in the spotlight is short.

But the mess didn't begin at the Mill. The foundation for the slam was a series at the old Get Me High Lounge, where Marc founded a poetry reading series in 1984. Wanting to avoid the owl-rimmed glasses, tweed jackets, and relentless droning of the academic stage and the drunken spittle of the typical barroom bard, Marc emphasized performance and the capture of audience.

By the time he was approached by Dave Jemilo, the Green Mill's owner, two years later—to help inject a bit of sizzle into slow Sunday nights—the ex-construction worker had the blueprint. Stanzas and spirits were a potent mix. Obstinate judges and teeny cash prizes made things interesting. The word *slam* sounded brisk, relentless, and final, something that couldn't be argued with. The limelight felt great on Marc's skin. A star was born. A phenomenon found root.

Marc presided over the buzz like a blade-edged Svengali. He decided who was legit, who wore the fever like a cloak, and who was there just to beef up their social circle, drink heavily, and talk in the back of the bar while poets were onstage. He never apologized for running the world inside the threshold of the Mill. Often he was gruff and unreadable. He was stubborn. He was frequently brilliant. At the risk of being ostracized by black folks and ridiculed by white ones, I never told anyone what an astounding presence he was and is in my life. I'd never met anyone so selfishly and selflessly fueled by language and ego. I shamelessly clamored for a spot under his wing, where I wrote like a woman possessed, learned how to control any room with words, and inherited a bit of his swagger and arrogance—just enough to grow the thick skin needed to face a restless room of strangers every week.

There are two types of people in the world. The first are people who try the slam once and are absolutely horrified from the moment they take the stage. They leave skid marks running away from the experience. They forget that it's a crapshoot, that the judges' qualifications are simply (a) they are in the room, and (b) they are willing to be judges. From the time they skedaddle from the spotlight, these folks are content to watch the chaos from the sidelines. They're glad they dipped their toes in the water—it is a badge of honor of sorts—but they will never approach the mic again. The judging aspect of the slam proves to be more wounding than it looks. The aspiring wordsmiths make the common mistake of believing that a low score means that their poetry stank. They reveal much more than they thought they would. Or all those expectant eyes are just too . . . expecting.

The other type of person slams and discovers a surprising and mildly unsettling competitive streak. When I first hit that room, clutching my two or three poems, the local Green Mill slam champion was a woman named Lisa Buscani, a wizard who worked miracles by holding whole audiences in her hand. It was for her that I first used the word *diva*. When she finished a poem, there would be a moment of white-hot silence—audience members were so flummoxed, they didn't know whether to clap or weep. I'd never seen anyone wield that type of power over an entire room. I wanted to know if she did it by telling her own stories. I wanted to know how she did it.

But Lisa's not the person who introduced me to the idea of the second throat.

We all have one. Our first throat is functional, a vessel for the orderly progression of verb, adjective, and noun. It's the home of our practiced, public voices. But most people live all their lives without discovering the second throat, that raw and curving parallel pathway we use to sing the songs, tell the stories, screech the truths that any fool knows should be kept silent.

Before I knew there was a slam, before Marc Smith set my complacency ablaze, I knew there was an audience somewhere and that something inside me ached to connect to it, to open that second throat and singe the air. Even the hard syllable and inferred violence of the word *slam* reminds me of how completely and irrevocably my world was changed because of one moment, one woman, one atypical Chicago night.

It was a signature blend of Chi-town chaos, with all the elements in attendance. Alcohol? Yes. The blues? The place was drenched in them. Insanely subpar temperature outside and a bellowing wind clawing at the doorframe, begging to get in? You betcha.

In January 1988, in the fledging days of slam, forty poets came together at Blues Etc., a raucous juke joint on the city's North Side. They were there for Neutral Turf, a benefit for Guild Books, a venerable and funky literary institution and one of those places that was always in some stage of revolt.

Ten bucks got you more than three dozen word-slingers in a blues club for four hours over the course of a blistering late winter afternoon—you couldn't ask for more Chicago than that. Well, yeah, you could—that same ten bucks got you into a performance of the Johnny B. Moore Blues Band later that evening. The place was packed. In true Windiest City style, it wasn't just the place we were. It felt like the only place to be.

When I walked into that blues club on that January afternoon, I was one of those people fully prepared to get mildly (okay, not so mildly) buzzed and to laugh at funny people saying funny things onstage. I was prepared for poetry of the June-moon-spoon-spittoon variety, grade-school rhymes delivered with grown-up earnestness. Real poetry, I felt, was inescapably dull, necessarily inaccessible, relegated to dusty, high-up bookshelves, buried in tomes that opened with a reluctant creak. Real poetry certainly wasn't real poetry if you could understand it. Real poetry was about the universe revealed in the defiant way a flower bursts through a crack in the concrete. Real poetry mused about maddeningly cryptic quotes from deities. Real poetry was written by alcoholic white men in musty tweed jackets or their anorexic, suicidal female counterparts. I didn't know much about poetry, obviously, but I had heard somewhere that a woman poet had taken her life by sticking her head in an oven and gulping mouthfuls of gas. You had to be a real poet to do that.

Neutral Turf was designed to be a space and time for the city's disparate creative elements to commune, connect, raise a glass or two, and discover—well, I'll be damned—that their work was crafted on a common canvas. An academic stepped gingerly down from his ivory tower to hear poetry penned on a scarred bar top by an edgy artist. A painfully shy high school sophomore listened to Luis Rodriguez and recognized a little of himself. People who had never picked up a poetry book or strolled into a college classroom heard Michael Anania, whose work was featured in the *Norton Anthology of Modern Poetry*; Reginald Gibbons, the editor of the prestigious lit journal *TriQuarterly*; and Lisel Mueller, who would snag a Pulitzer ten years later. There were rants, villanelles, poets reciting from memory. Marc Smith, just another stranger at the mic, wailed his fiery odes to the rafters, and possibility was static in the air.

With my jaw on the floor, I listened while boundaries blurred, lines were definitively crossed, walls crumbled. Those attending their very first poetry reading (many, like me, initially attracted by the booze, the four hours of guaranteed warmth, and the opportunity—they thought—to publicly guffaw at reams of bad rhyme) got an enviable sampling of everything the city's poetry community had to offer.

But that formidable chasm between the poets from academia and those with street cred wasn't the only one being bridged that day.

Chicago's dirty little secret is the blatant segregation lurking directly beneath its midwestern charm. Blacks, comprising more than 30 percent of the city's population, live primarily on the West and South Sides. Whites huddle on the North Side. Hispanics, southwest and northwest. The practice of herding minorities toward particular economically stifled areas of the city, fueled by fear and good ole garden-variety racial prejudice, took hold in the late 1800s. At the beginning of the next century, thousands of Delta residents streamed northward, searching for the blessings of the city, and settled into those same areas where faces and perspectives mirrored their own. That "comfort around my own kind" took root and continues today, effectively reinforcing the borders and earning Chicago—which produced the first African American president—the title of the most segregated city in America.

Any Chicago native can recite the rules. Stay out of Garfield Park and Lawndale. No black folks allowed in Cicero or Bridgeport or Berwyn, unless they're going to or coming from work. Englewood? Gangs. Wrong or right, lines drawn long ago are still etched in the minds of the city's residents, and the poetry community traveled along those same lines. North Side poets (mostly white) and South Side poets (mostly black) not only rarely mingled but also tended to sniff rather dismissively at one another. And the West Side? Poetry? Could there have been any poetry at all in those abandoned apartment buildings, rusty park swings, and block after block of taverns, storefront churches, and fly-by-night commerce?

Poets in Chicago felt possessive of their stories. Neighborhoods were starkly defined, each with its own defiant character, quirky ritual, and local folklore. Neighborhoods were kielbasa, black-eyed peas, Vienna red hots, chitlins, or cannoli. Neighborhoods were towers of public housing, sturdy two-flats, or manicured McMansions. Just like everyone else, poets love that *boing* of instant recognition; they love being surrounded by people who have lived the same stories they have. Outside of that warm circle, there was a glaring mistrust of the "other." What will you do with my stories? How can I hand them over to be interpreted by you, a stranger, someone whose skin, history, environment, and outlook are different from mine?

On that long-ago winter night, Blues Etc. was filled with folks from the West Side, the North Side, and the South Side, suppressing their doubts and spinning their tales across boundaries. The night's klutzy harmonics marked a first for Chicago's creative community—it was a ragged ballad sung by the whole city at once.

And *she* sat there, amid the frenetic swirl, watching as stanza after stanza stepped to the mic. Many times, she looked as if the poet on stage was a child of hers—she nodded with a mixture of patience and bemused pride at the occasional overworked rhyme, mumbled delivery, or tangled syntax. She glowed when a passage touched her and seemed about to reach out and touch those poets whose work probed deeply and reached bone. She laughed in all the right places and served up compassion when it was called for—stopping every now and again to push up slipping-down coke-bottle specs with her forefinger, adjust her heavy winter stockings, or graciously acknowledge an awestruck admirer.

For hours she defied the odds, front row center, rapt and nurturing during what amounted to the longest, most eclectic reading ever. And when she was finally introduced, those who hadn't recognized her dropped their jaws in amazement, and those who had known she was there all along thanked the Muse that they were among those huddled in the club on that day, at that moment. She unfolded her body slowly and stood up to amble to the stage, where she turned to face those who had already spoken and those who had come to listen. They were C-minus students and ex-cons, pump jockeys, middle-school teachers, drunks and bag boys, black folks from Lawndale and white folks from Schaumburg, word addicts, coke addicts, Wicker Park and Winnetka, slammers, GEDers and grad students, academics, dropouts, Baptists and Buddhists, lone wolves and prizewinners.

And she was Gwendolyn Brooks.

When you hear the phrase *Chicago poetry*, the scene-stealing poetry slam begins its low relentless roar and barges in to hog the limelight. The raucous, controversial competition—the brash Olympics of lyric—drew its first breath in the Windy, which of course makes perfect sense when one considers the blustery, sexy beast it's become. The slam is constantly rediscovered and dissected, lauded and loathed, and has gradually risen to the level of idle cocktail party fodder for those who wish to appear "in." Unfortunately, simply hearing Chicago poetry causes some folks' synapses to fire wrongly and insanely, and the slam becomes the city's creative community. Was there a community before the slam, and did one come after? Was the slam itself birthed by a larger, more ambitious community? Who knows? It's easier to succumb to that handy catchphrase overwhelming everything, much easier to slather the whole wall with that bright-red paint.

There is an official history of poetry slam, as well as several unofficial ones. There are exaggerations and outright lies to be had for the asking. There are painstakingly researched timelines that feature all the major players and defining moments. It's simple to find out that the first poetry slam at the Green Mill was held on July 25, 1986, that the first national competition was in the fall of 1990, and who was there and how the competition caught fire from that instance. For some, the proceedings were nothing more than a unique, booze-fueled recreation; for others, like myself, the slam became necessary breath.

I went on to snag the stats—four individual championships, the most in the competition's history—and became, arguably of course, one of the slam's most recognizable and successful competitors. But, as slam's defenders are fond of saying, "the points are not the point." I believe that those of us who flourished during those first heady days brought unfinished voices and bare need to the table. For many of us, those voices had their beginning in some other arena, in some other room.

For me, it was that singular moment when a regal, bespectacled colored lady stood before that ragtag cross-section of the city's poets and poetry lovers. If I hadn't seen her there, I might never have discovered that poetry held answers for me. It was that stark moment when the glasses stopped clinking, the chatter stilled, and we held a familial breath, waiting for her. It was that unforgettable moment that still, for me, typifies the breadth and strength of the Chicago poetry community. I didn't know it at the time, but the slam's boisterous brilliance was made possible because it found a city that was finally ready for it. And because, in so many ways, writers were finding a need and needing an answer.

And remember that community of black folks and rusty park swings, abandoned apartment buildings, and block after desolate block of taverns, storefront churches, and fly-by-night commerce? The poetry-starved West Side of the city? During the Great Migration of blacks from south to north, when my mother came up from Alabama and my father came up from Arkansas, they settled on the West Side. That's where I was born, where I grew up.

Needless to say, when I set out for Blues Etc., intent on a little cultural entertainment, I didn't expect that anyone there would know, or understand, the stories I held close while I searched for the voice I needed to tell them. Although my public motto was "People who say they're passionate about writing should write in as many ways as possible," I didn't hold out much hope that poetry could offer a West Side colored girl any real resolution, consolation, or guidance.

Until a South Side colored girl stood up and began to speak. Gwendolyn Brooks, who I knew was from Chicago, who I knew was famous, who I knew had won a big writing award or two, who I knew—well, from photographs. Somewhere along the line, I'd memorized her poem "The Pool Players. Seven at the Golden Shovel," which I, like everyone else I knew, assumed was titled "We Real Cool." I thought of her as a comfy homegrown attraction, more as a local personality than a poet, someone who had slipped through a slit in the canon of moody alcoholic white men and their suicidal female counterparts.

In a voice that was warm, crisp, and encompassing, she told snippets of story that belonged to us both. She knew the cluttered neighborhood streets, the tenement apartments, the forgotten schools. In her I sensed the black-girl uncertainty, the gangliness, the ache of never quite belonging. I suddenly saw myself there, emboldened under the hot lights, holding the attention of a room full of people who I never thought realized my existence. Gwen Brooks didn't capture that room with histrionics or trendy wordplay. All she had were her stories and a naked need to have them heard and understood. I realized that nothing mattered as much as having a room full of strangers invest in my story in just that way—and helping them find ways to tell stories of their own.

✶ ✶ ✶ ✶

So we stepped out on the huge stage of the Chicago Theater, Marc, Cin, Dean, and I, and looked out at the past and future of slam. Folks who had sweated out the particulars during those first days, who had helped Marc map out rules we could break, seemed a little overwhelmed. New blood, alternately wary and cocky, scanned the hoopla, dying to be seen. Morley Safer was still in awe. These were poets, after all.

Before we began our poem, the four of us listened as our names were shouted from the audience. Chicago was claiming its own. I was a fool to think it had forgotten us.

We rooted ourselves, waited for silence, then opened our second throats.

Somewhere in the back of the theater, my muse smiled and slipped out the back door. She was wearing coke-bottle specs and stockings pulled to a roll just beneath her knees.

GROUND ZERO

UPTOWN MONOLOGUE

To the east the moving waters as far as the eye can follow. To the west . . .

Broadway, Lawrence, the Aragon Ballroom, the Riviera dance club, the boarded-up Uptown Theatre, Bud Lite Betty, Slime Corner, the Saxony, Shake Rattle and Read, and Fiesta Cooking.

In 1857 this was a prairie! . . . No, this was a forest! . . . No, this was a mosquito-infested bog until the railroads came on the east and the railroads came on the west hauling with them Germans and Swedes and Irishmen with hammers in their pockets, nails in their mouths, and know-how in their potato-famine brains. And with that know-how, supplemented by lumber shamelessly stripped from Michigan shores by Yankee Doodle East Coast dandies, they erected between those two fledging railroads—one elevated on the east, one running the ridge on the west—they erected two-flats, hundreds and hundreds of two-flats, which gave way and were torn down to make way for three-flats and four-flats and soon multilevel multiflats. Too many flats for the scales of the music. Totally blue from one point of view.

And to fill up the flats the trains coughed out people. Wayward people. Gotta get away people. People who wanted to rest. Restless people. People with a push and a hello. People who wouldn't say nothin'. Nothin' people. And people who had everything and wanted more.

They filled up the flats and the flats rose higher. They came from everywhere. Poland. Czechoslovakia. Peoria. Kalamazoo. In throngs they came from Kentucky. Displaced miners from Tennessee. West Virginians like our old friend Mr. Casey Jones, who used to say,

> When you're down and out
> Raise your head high
> And shout,
> OH SHIT!

They filled in the bog and the bog brimmed over. The hotels became halfway houses. The street glittered with the litter of shattered glass. The well heeled watched from their towers along the lakeshore as the cars burned and the disenfranchised hurled rocks through their own windows.

Uptown! The Heart of Uptown! And the Mill where Hanks and Phils and Eddies once powwowed together on the bandstand to pass the mad dog around in a circle. Where once you could purchase any experience you could conjure up in your sick mind from a fantastic him, her, or it emerging from the Hisez or Herzez. Where a misplaced "fuck you" could bring cold steel trouble through the small of your back and without knowing it you were violence in a way few men or women get to know violence cut by its quick matter-of-fact routine blink-of-an-eye brutality.

Uptown! Where if you stood in one place too long you got shuffled aside by the next new entries into this North Shore port of hog-butcher dreams. Where the crank of material progress machinating out of the octopi capital gains pukes up heads and hearts onto homeless shores blown out by the windbags of possibility; where human hurricanes of vice and self-destruction fight each other each day over petty scams and cheap pleasures while the well heeled, accommodated in their towers along the lakeshore, commiserate the misery from a safe distance as they listen to the tick tick tick of their ticker tapes as they tickle their manicured toes.

And now what has come to this low point along the lakeshore to once again fill in the rotted pockets? What is this latest migration—perhaps the most dangerous of all?

Poets!
Jazz musicians!
Artistes!
Oh God help us now!

And they too have come from faraway places. Places with strange exotic names like Schaumburg . . . Palatine . . . Buffalo Grove.

Among them are the you-read-it-I'm-scared poets. The come with a sour puss on their faces let's see what this slam is all about poets. The I'm alone will anybody talk to me there poets. The living in the streets poets. The who haven't written a word in their lives poets. The could be poets. The I'm gonna be great poets. The nobody poets. The never will be poets. The you and I, what everybody says is what we all say poets.

They're all here and you're here too. It's Sunday night at the Green Mill. You're at the slam, the original slam, and I'm the one who started them all. My name is Marc Smith.

"SO WHAT!"

NO EXIT SUNDAY

Two hours and ten minutes until time tells me I've got to do it all again at the Green Mill, and I'm suckin' down coffee nonstop at the No Exit Café watchin' Bert the Bass Player tune his fiddle twistin' the keys at the top of the neck as smoke curls 'round his postbeatnik head. Count Drumula tightens his snare, taps the tom-tom, throws a goatee smile across the room lockin' me in its Pepsodent cage.

It's the midafternoon jazz set on Sunday and I've been drainin' coffee from the pot-bottomless in the back corner between the Go boards like a pill popper tryin' to escape into some other state of being having been here . . . there . . . or wherever-the-fuck-I-am too long turnin' my thoughts over and over again in that endless arcade of funny-house mirrors known as the Psycho Babble Halls of Self-Deluded Introspection.

And after three more cups, black, heaped with sugar, I've come to the conclusion that the world is moving too fast! It's speed-percolating! Everybody's gone nuts! Nobody's got a clue. If you need proof, pick up a newspaper. Read it!

MEN SLAPPIN' BABIES INTO BAGS OF LIMP FLESH

MAMAS TOSSIN' TODDLERS OUT OF WINDOWS

SOMEBODY PROPOSING A PLAN TO PRIVATIZE SPACE

HOODOOS SLAUGHTERIN' VOODOOS

MACHETE-TOTIN' TEACHERS
CHOPPIN' UP THEIR STUDENTS

TALK SHOW TELEHOSTS
TELLIN' THE WORLD HOW TO THINK

HAIL BOB! THE COMET!
LAY DOWN AND DRINK
SOME FAR-OUT
JONESDAY COOL AID

NUTS! That's what the world is NUTS!

Finnerty slips a reed into the stem of his saxophone, moistens it, and counts off *two three four*. Drumula hits. Soto jumps in. Bert couples up. And we take the A Train into yet another Night in Tunisia draggin' our dumb souls along Green Dolphin Street.

Look! The clock has moved another inch. It is now twenty-eight minutes until hit time and I don't want to do it no more! I don't want to face them with my happy manic face. Nuts! All of us are nuts! Doin' the things we don't want to do right on schedule! Why? What's the reason for it anyway?

One last cup and I'm out the door, up the street, in the car headin' south for Stella in the corner Starlight, chasin' the A Train along Sheridan, disembarking on Broadway, my not so giant footsteps indenting the sidewalk snowpack.

I look down at my feet, newsprint stuck in the ice, and wonder, "Whose shoes are these anyway?"

NOBODY'S HERE

All the world in another place.
All the flashing lights
On the city slick
Pointing somewhere
But not here.

Hit the jukebox, Donnie!

Put some dollars in its throat.
Hang us around
For one more smoky hour
Of *I want you* conversation.
Dreams runnin' down the Old Style bottles
Like tears down somebody's cheek.

Quarters in the jukebox, Donnie!

Tell all the passed-over dreamers who wanna know
That somewhere some starlight Daddy
Hops atop the telephone lines
Above this gray and obscure city
Poppin' his fingers makin' the moon jump,
Makin' a comet's tail
Spin out of a stone axe grinding
On a wheel shootin' sparks
Into the dead black sky.
Ridin' a train of lights
On rails that scream
Midnight . . . Two . . . and Four a.m.

Tellin' us all to go back,
Go back to somewhere
Even if we don't know where that is.

So, hit the jukebox, Donnie!
Let all the songs play out.
    Ring the last call bell, Tom!
Turn the lights up.
    Shake the loveless hearts alive again,
       Lois.
Send them off to home
To sleep another night alone
    'Cause nobody's here.
    Nobody's here.

GROUND ZERO

It don't matter me no way no how.
I'm right here smack-dab in the middle.
So no way it's gonna matter to me.
And I ain't diggin' no concrete coffin,
No back yard mausoleum
To keep me a pickle sweet a plenty
Plied with sardines and pork sausage wieners
Livin' out the chance that some bubble-flesh victim
Will come puckered up and scabby lipped
To kiss me in the name of a new mankind.

Oh no! Not me, Big Bro.
I want that radio transmitter nuclear guidance system
Stuck right here in my pocket.
Better yet stitch the thing under my skin.
I want the First World Third World East West
Bagdad Beirut Korea Tehran
To tune in, lock on, and lift off!

And before I make like the vapors,
Before I say hello there   Flash!   Good-bye!
I'm gonna run like Walter Payton
Transcontinental
With one of those long bullets
Building speed behind me.
I'm gonna jump rivers
Like a king colossal Jesse Owens.
I'm going to hurdle cities like . . . like . . .
Like whoever hurdles.

Beep beepin' and zoom zoomin'
Scrabblin' the midair early alerts
Bustin' through the sandbag barricades

Topplin' the do not enters
Zigzaggin' the checkpoint Charlie zebras—
A crazy-legged jack fool with a twenty megaton shadow
Beep beepin' as he crisscrosses sprinklers swishin' lawns
Trampling down the manicured hedgerows
Pourin' on the speed as he heads up his
Hallelujah! Touchdown drive!
For the you'll never make it if I don't
Bay window alongside the rose garden
Outside that whitest house of all!

Hopin' that some auspicious occasion
Has got just about every politician
On this soon to be gone face of the earth
Eating caviar like balloon heads
At the longest table in the world.
Just cautious enough. Just conservative enough
To consider ten seconds of protocol
Before making the inquiry,

"Say George, who is that out there
dashing across the lawn?"

Why it's . . . ME!
Runnin' the last fifty yards at low altitude
Toward their face-fillin' detent
Boy this sure looks good
Banquet inside the checkerboard mullions
Which I crash through
Checking the wizards of world peace and power
Eye to eye as I belly slide atop the table
Spewing beef stroganoff and vichyssoise onto their tuxedos
Casting my final ballot in their careers of being someplace else safe
When the ball's up in the air comin' down down down
Beepin' like holy fire tearin' the skin loose from their bones!

Me! Finally havin' my day! Me!
Finally havin' my say!

Me! Slidin' up to the five star director of all this crap.
      The hardware only seconds behind.
Me! Cryin' into their bewildered something fucked-up faces,

> *"Beep Beep Beep! Boom Zoom! Boys!*
> *Take this one and bank it in Switzerland!"*

ASSHOLE ON HIS CELL PHONE SHOUTING

The first indication that there was a problem (*and a poem brewing*) was the incoming electric sounds that went through a series of tonal transformations beginning with a rattling alarm clock and passing on to a synthesized rotary dial ring ring ring ring that screamed,

"Answer me! Answer me! Answer me!"

Of course, he didn't. He allowed the ring to morph into a second stage of notification. Whistle whines. Disco soundscapes bouncing from wall to wall while he balanced his latte and cheesecake on a bright red removable bicycle seat.

"And they're off!"

Followed by a horse-race bugle trumpeted so forcefully that you could almost see the clay fly up from the hooves of a dozen thoroughbreds stampeding through clouds of cigar smoke circling the heads of a half dozen handicappers hunched over the rail.

And then a second race was announced . . . and a third!

HELLO BOBBY?
BOBBY? IS THAT YOU?
HEY, WHERE ARE YOU?
YEAH YEAH YEAH!
NO! NO! NO!
YOU'VE GOT IT WRONG!
YOU'RE COMING FROM DOWNTOWN!
GO NORTH!
NINETY FOUR NORTH!
YEAH!
LOOK FOR THE SIGNS.
FULLERTON TO DAMEN
LAKE SHORE DRIVE.

LAKE SHORE DRIVE!
BY THE LAKE!
TELL ME AGAIN,
WHERE ARE YOU NOW?
LOOK AT THE SIGNS!

I'm over here, motherfucker,
Two tables away.

IF ALL ELSE FAILS JUST KNOW
YOU'RE SOUTH OF ME.
THAT'S RIGHT SOUTH.
AND YOU HAVE TO GO NORTH!
'CAUSE YOU'RE SOUTH.
THAT'S RIGHT. YOU'RE SOUTH
ABOUT FIFTEEN MINUTES—
FIFTEEN MINUTES AWAY.

"Hey! . . . HEY!"
But he can't hear me.
He can't even hear himself
Causing me to wonder
Whether a *bullet* would stop him?

OKAY, I'LL BE WAITING OUTSIDE.
OUTSIDE THE BREW AND STEW.
THAT'S WHAT IT'S CALLED
THE BREW AND STEW!
SOUTH SIDE OF THE STREET.
THAT'S RIGHT.
FIFTEEN MINUTES.
YOU'RE FIFTEEN MINUTES AWAY!

LOOK, I'M GONNA HANG UP NOW.
PEOPLE ARE GETTING ANNOYED.
YEAH! RIGHT!
FIFTEEN MINUTES . . .
NO FOURTEEN NOW.
SEE YOU.

Would one bullet do it? No. I'd have to empty a clip into him like Rambo. Become a folk hero. The guy who silenced the Asshole Screaming on His Cell Phone. It would mean the end of my freedom. The end of my opportunity to enjoy my easy life of typing gripes into a laptop at swanky cafés witnessing and recording the wonders of modern American culture and technology. But it would be so worth it to hear his last

BYE! CIAO! LATER!

WINTER CAFÉ

Reading the newspaper a woman sips her soup.
Her eyes never leave the newsprint.
She breaks a cracker, cleans the spoon,
Gulps her coffee, turns the page—
All animated against a steamed-up window
In a café at the corner of . . .

Behind her, as if riding on a train,
A man in an oversized overcoat
Counts out his pennies into a brown cross.
Counts them once. Counts them twice.
Counts them over and over again,
Coffee and roll in front of him.

Through the doorway enters Janet.
Blond, bitter, badly broken—
A bombshell somebody dropped in a forgotten field.
Fake fur coat. Shredded nylons.
Sunglasses riding on an overpowdered nose.
She lights a cigarette
And the room retreats
From her tortured inquisition:

> *Why don't you just . . . just . . .*
> *Why don't you just . . . just . . .*

Down the block and across the street
A bus throws up slush
At the feet of a motley band of travelers
Who jump back from leaning out to looksee
As a salt truck swings its blade
Ferociously around the corner
Popping sparks off the pavement,
Tossing nuggets over the curb.

Why don't you just . . . just . . .
Why don't you just . . . just . . .

George, the greasy Greek, spins a plate of stuffed chops
To a perfect landing atop the stainless steel hot plate counter
Where they glow in the orange light of the heat lamp
Until Mable with the hanging jowls
Fetches them with a frown
Drowning them in her drawl
As she hauls them haphazardly over to Leon
Who hollers something to Louie
Who laughs at Boyle
Who rings the cash register
And counts out three dollars and some change
To Louise
Who stares at Janet
Still raging onstage near the doorway.

Why don't you just . . . just . . .
Why don't you just . . . just . . .

"WHY DON'T YOU JUST WHAT?" bawls out Brian
Pulling up his pants, tightening his belt
Comin' out of the toilet cussin'
'Cause he's had enough of dis
        "BULLSHIT!"
        And he's goin' home
"HEAR THAT!   HOME!"

Which might make some sense
If he had one.

FACE ON THE FLOOR

Look down at it. Look at it!
Shaping the hexagons in this porcelain room.
A finger game.
See Mommy Daddy. Do Mommy Daddy.

I said, look at it.
Look down at it,
A face so much a part of the pattern
That all you have to do is squeeze your eyes
And it's you
Head at the base of the water closet
Cheek and eye rubbing the floor.
Cotton lips. Damp skin.
Rocking Rocking.
Mommy Daddy see. See Mommy Daddy . . .

Oh please do look at it
Running its fingers along the grouted joints
Finger-painting the tiles,
Drawing pictographs that say,
"Look at me. Look at what I've become.
The brown soup I lay my face in.
The stink smeared on the floor.
The 'oh no oh no oh no.'

"Look at me!
I'm your floor. You're my floor.
We live for the floor
Tightening our stomachs with guttural moan,
Tracing and retracing the patterns,
Splattering our lives like dizzy morning
                echoes   echoes   echoes
That stick to the bowl."

Mommy-Daddies see what Mommy-Daddies see.
And Mommy-Daddies do what Mommy-Daddies do.

THE SIGN RATTLED
IT HAD ALL THESE BUTTONS OF GLASS

Stanley's store at the end of our alley
Had a dead end sign shaped like a diamond
Set into the ground at the back of the curb
Turned up on a point,
One of its kind left in the world.

Euclid Avenue ran into it.
Eighty-Fourth Place crossed it.
Tootie-Fruitie Freddie and Ricky Cooke
Pitched pennies on the sidewalk behind it.
I raced Kenny Knottingham
In a race I regarded
As the race of my life
From the blotched beige bark
Of the big-leaf sycamore, peeling
To within a tag-hand's reach of winning
Rattling the buttons of glass
That covered the sign
As I fell to the ground.
A hand on the curb.
A hand in the mud.
My face scraped by the pipe
That supported that sign.

It was the race of my life   Lost
Boarded up   Abandoned
Block by block purchased and sold.
And try as I may not to
I run it again and again.
Sometimes in my dreams.
Sometimes while sipping coffee in North Shore cafés
Or on the Gold Coast

When the autumn dusk drops its lavender haze
And the electric lights in the buildings
Square themselves double on the damp streets
Making the people I do not know
Weave in and out of the mist
To become the people I forgot to keep with me
Walking out of my mind
Into places that will never be again.

Stanley's store at the end of our alley.
A pane of glass framing another world.
A dead end sign.
And a race I run backwards
Never able to win.

PYROMANIAC

Eyes burn.
Hands and knees hot.
Sun stone spinning.
A spot
Where the Slo Poke broke
And hit the burnt grass.
Down on his knees
Alvin lit cruel pools
Of liquid fuels
Around anthill agonies.

Alvie, come in and have some soup.
Bozo's on.

Eating the sidewalk fire
Alvin pressed his face
Closer to the earth
To see and study
One ugly hour
Of noon's terrible heat.
Ant and ant eternal energy anguishing.
The Slo Poke treat in flames.
Death games that pass the empty afternoons.
Ant wars.
Lighter fluid into holes.

Alvie, please come in.

Baits of butterscotch and cream,
Screams sandlike small,
And regiments inanely formed
To battle a horrible god
Whose feet encompass colonies

And fingers twitch to touch
With sugar torched sensations
Bodies of ants
Caked onto kerosene candies.

Alvie, your soup's getting cold.

BALLPARK POEM

I'm sitting on a fire hydrant halfway between my forty-fifth and forty-sixth season enhancing my tan while I wait for my pals to arrive with the tickets.

Peanuts!

And a street vendor leaning against a blond brick wall fifty feet beyond the center field fence cries,

Peanuts!

Sounding somewhat like a cricket because the squall he makes is louder than his body should allow.

Peanuts!

Three cops sitting sidesaddle on a blue horse, side arms bulging out conspicuously, adjust their doughnut bellies as they chitchat, takin' it easy on their fair weather patrol.

Peanuts!

Ten Wichita, Kansas, corn-fed bullheads plug up the intersection hunting for Gate F. The cop nearest the traffic jam reluctantly does his duty with a groaning eyeball roll,

"Down there, sir. Gate F is down there
Where the big F is."

Peanuts!

People plash by in streams of placid pastels. Pops and his buzz-head kids, Wendy and hers, Bertha and what could be children but what may be baby hippopotami tuggin' at their mama as they lumber across the street linked together hand to hand, the last one dragging an antique catcher's mitt.

Peanuts!

From the top of the plug I shoot my scanner out into the loveliness of lots and lots of ladies, dolls, and dames. Over-forty me can't help being a pig sometimes, especially at the ballpark. Hell, when I'm out here I'm like a WGN cameramen zoomin' in on

Peanuts!

Some bad habits are hard to kick.

Anyway, I spot a peroxide blond wearing a pink halter top, eating a Polish sausage at the beer stand across the street, making lipstick autographs on the bun. I fantasize that she's signing it for me.

Peanuts!

"Got tickets?"

Something tries to invade my daydream.

Peanuts!

"Got tickets?"

It starts to dissolve.

Peanuts!

"I said, d'ya got tickets?"

Is this my friend?

"Hey! I'm talkin' to you!"

Not my friend.

24

"All you got to say is yes or no.
You people.
You people and your looks."

It's a hawk, a hustler, a young man scalping a fist of fake tickets. He's tough, muscular, feral, Red Dog dago tee. His eyes peg me reactively. I feel my own opaque glare matching up to his. For a second we stare coldly into each other's eyes.

"All I asked you was if you had tickets.
And if you do, just say no thank you.
Save me the hard-guy look."

Peanuts!

"You people.
When are you people
Ever gonna stop
Lookin' down at us?"

Peanuts!

"You don't own this street."

Peanuts!

"And you don't own me."

Peanuts!

"And if you don't have the guts
To say what you're thinkin',
Then don't parade around
As if you got the guts to do anything else."

Peanuts!

"You people."

Down the block and across the street Big Mama leans over the porch rail and hollers, "Ramon! Ramon!" who runs up to the cricket on the corner, holdin' out a handful of money, cryin',

"Peanuts! Peanuts!

I want some peanuts!"

You got 'em little buddy. They're all yours. Take 'em home.
Take 'em home and enjoy yourself. Enjoy eating your

Peanuts!

CONGA BEAT

At the Bucktown Art Fair   Chicago 1986

Black thunder crack-flappin' angelic wings
Smack the skins angling out.
The lady with her brown bag bread
Circles round, circles 'bout.
Which way you goin' babushka head?

Smart kid skateboard flips and turns.
Push foot fast, he glides away.
All scatter
When the storm winds batter
The artsy-fartsy Buck Town show.

Kathy wraps up her photos.
Raoul guzzles the wine.
Old Glory waves on a canvas.
And the kids are screamin' somewhere.
Yeah, the kids are screamin' somewhere.

But it's come upon us cool and fast,
Big drops poundin' the street.
Breezes whippin' the newsprint 'round.
The downbeat kicks.
The downbeat kicks and flips
      the spirit
         of a man gone cool
    in the middle of the park
      playing his conga
    with no questions asked
Playin' the . . .

Beat soul sound,
The sound of a gentle movement of a kiss,
The sound of embracing stars.

Man reigns.
Rain runs down.
Rain runs down through his fingers,
      through the headwind sound moving east,
      through the sound of the sunset burnin' death,
      through the sound of the sunset
          Red   Red   **RED!**

The man   gone cool
      in the middle of the park
Plays his conga
Makin' orange scenes of yellow steam
Rise up from the puddles after the rain.

He plays the conga.
He plays the conga.
Play Conga!

BRADLEY MORTON

One of my few grammar-school victories came early in the first semester of the third grade. Out on the playground under the October sun, I flipped the rotundus Bradley Morton, judo-style, landing him flat on his back, making drab little dust puffs cloud out from the slag ash under his two-by-four butt.

Wherever you are now, Bradley, I owe you!

You were my primo victim, my first opportunity to be just as much an infantile brute as all the other hyperactive schoolyard ninjas stalking the third grade recess circles.

Bradley, I remember how politely you stood there, big as a small house, extending me your soft white dough boy hand, grinning as you placed it into my gritty grip waiting for the cause and effect to follow.

There was no anger in our experiment.

We were simply testing an ancient jujitsu theory . . . how a small force with the right leverage can overthrow massive opposition.
And when I hefted you up onto my hip, heaving your anatomy higher and higher, more aloft than either one of us thought possible—your wrist twisted, your eyes widening, your mouth a pronounced

"Oh!"

There was no malice in my heart, Bradley. Honest!

We were just playing out our parts in that time-everlasting ritual of hero and hunted, conquest and conqueror.

Bless my soul, Bradley, I had no idea how right the jujitsu grandfathers would be.

Flipping you, flying arms outstretched through the crisp autumnal air, was an unexpected feat Colossal!

And when you fell, like thunder to the earth, eyes watering, tears slipping out of their squinting slits, I wanted to lift you into my arms, Bradley, cradle you, and kiss your rosy cheeks pleading to be forgiven.

But you were too damn big, Bradley.
And me so very small.

COCKREN

I first met Cockren downstairs in the utility room of the First Presbyterian Church on west Addison. He had a head like mushmelon, a huge petrified mushmelon with beady piglike eyes floating in two spoon scoops above a withered cucumber snout. All stuck onto a fleshy beer-barrel torso with creamy elongated gourds flapping out the shirt sleeves. I didn't like looking at him. And I liked him less when he opened his mouth. He was a bar fight ready to break glass over some petty incident.

Look,
I can see from the crooked direction of your nose
That you've mixed it up a little.
Well, don't be fooled, I have too.
Push me to too-far
And I'll push back.
Back into the grandstand postures
And the two-by-four equalizers
That can lay a hunk of human meat
Down flat with no avenue out.

You see,
After my nights out there
Mixing bad blood
At least I had the sense
To twist the bones back
Into a position presentable
For public viewing.

You and your broken mug
Still broadcast trouble.

It was a testimony to how little we know about life's undercurrent of irony. Cockren and his mushmelon self became my cosmic buddy, my spiritual pilot, my Tuesday night take-home-dinner recipe of how one-on-one can sometimes be raised to the ultimate power and that's okay 'cause

> When the beady eyes soften in their ivory mist
> And the cut lips turn into a Frenchman's pout
> Old man Cockren
> Takes on the aura of a grease monkey Buddha,
> A one-line puncher God can't stop laughing at
> He who made the heavens
> Made this upside-down inside-out character
> From time to time almost as divine
> As the tears rolling down an old man's cheek.

Whenever Cockren and I glutted coffee at the Nugget discussing the condition of the Universe the topic always eventually swung back to his kids and the "fucked-up" society he had to raise them in. I could relate. My generation and his went through families and marriages and kids like toilet paper. Wipe it and throw it away. Houses, cars, toaster ovens . . . families.

Cockren's oldest suffered the most. His girls found a way through the mess via their mother. But Buck, the oldest, had taken too many hits. And all the amends, all the money, all the advice, all the after-the-fact guidance fixed nothing. Cockren watched his life resurface like a beer can bobbing along in a dirty river and he was helpless to do anything to about it.

"Here's one of the dumbest things I ever did. I still don't know what I had between my ears to think that this was something a father should do. I guess I wanted the kid to experience life in the raw or some goofed-up shit like that. It's hard to think back on this now.

"Am I boring you! Okay, it ain't that horrible. It's just one of those things that sticks.

"There's this apartment building at the end of the block, a twelve-flat. Not a real low-down bombed-out dump but a place where the transients come and go with a few hellos and no good-byes. It's Saturday morning, summertime. The squads are spinning their tops parked sideways in the wrong direction down the one-way street. The wife and the kids are bunched up on the porch with the nosey neighbors trying to get a good look at what's going down. It's bright outside. Beautiful. I remember that like it's today. Big clouds sailing across a blue sky. Gorgeous. The whole situation reminded me of the night a car ran over the fire hydrant in front of the Swede's place. 2 a.m. and the whole neighborhood is out in their pajamas watching the water shoot up like a geyser. Same situation when Old Fritz hung himself in the garage down the alley. These events put a stamp on ya.

"Anyway, here's what do I on that beautiful day. I take the kid down to the corner to see the transient guy all beat up bleeding on the stoop. He ain't dead, just drunk and busted up. But the kid, he's six years old! What's he thinking when he looks at this. I'll tell you what he's thinking. His imagination is thinking I'm lookin' at death and he don't even know what death is yet but he's lookin' at . . . in his head . . . in whatever instincts he's got about it. Death. Six years old. I make him look at it. What the fuck was the matter with me?

"And you know now that ain't the worst of it. Nope. Not at all. Minor league. When he's older I try apologizing. I'm going to fix it all up, see. Repair the damage. Mr. Fix-it. Guess what? He don't remember. Don't remember a goddamn thing. Laughs it off. Laughs at me!

"Stuffed it. We all do that. Make a long story short, growin' up he's afraid of everything, and then when he gets into the dope and the booze he goes the opposite direction. Every fuckin' evil shit you can imagine. God help somebody who thinks he knows what he's doing.

"Do you get what I'm tellin' ya?"

It's taken me a long time to understand Cockren's logic. I went over to his apartment one afternoon and there he was in the living with two sledgehammers duct-taped to the ends of an industrial broomstick doing bench presses on the sofa.

"Uh, why don't you just buy a set of weights or join a health club."

"I ain't that type. I don't join things. I don't want nobody looking into my business. I'm fifty-six years old. I ain't gonna be one of those high-class goofs riding a bicycle standing still. My old man would croak if he saw me at a health club."

"Uh, your old man did croak."

"He'd croak twice then."

Cockren's kid is in the music business. A show maker. House parties, raves, underground concerts. He's busted out a few times but keeps fighting back.

"The kid don't quit. I give him that. He'll lay down and get depressed for a day or two like the rest of us. Waste a week away maybe . . . Hey, I know you do too so don't pretend you don't. But the thing is you can only do that so long. Time runs out. He's thirty-three years old with nothing in the house to show for it. Hooks up with too many creeps that use him more than he can use them. The kid's generous to fault, selfish and generous at the same time. A fuckin' enigma.

"Here's the latest. He's been up all day for six nights straight. Probably poppin' bennies or whatever they call that crap now. Why? To put together a CD for one of his low-life buddies who could give two shits about all the work he's putting into their project. So fuckin' stoned they don't know their own names. I've seen 'em. They look like trash cans, smashed-up trash cans with legs and arms sticking out of the sides and mopheads hanging off the lids. I wanted to get a good grip on the junk hanging outta one guy's nose and give it a yank and let him know that if he fucks with the kid I'll lay him down like he ain't been laid down before.

"Guess what? He's a she. A broad big enough to kick my ass with her pinky finger. This is a fucked-up world. Let me tell ya.

"And these are the freaks he's doin' business with. Have you ever looked at the music they're playing on the TV? I'm sure you have. You're into all that goofy shit. You call it music. I call it evil. That's right. Evil. Look, I've done a lot of fucked-up crap in my life. Did it to the kids. Did it to the wife. To whole communities of people who didn't deserve it, but inside I knew I was fucked up. I had some guilt, however deep I hid it, and it ate away at me until I had to change. Don't be laughin' at me. I've changed. You wouldn't be sittin' here with me if the other guy was back.

"These shitheads think that the crap their doin' and sellin' on TV is some kind of answer, that it's okay, an alternative direction. It's fuckin' evil. Demon shit. The downward path. Hopeless. Cruel. And somebody should stand up and say that out loud so everybody can hear it.

"Are you followin' me?"

Buck and Cockren faced off one night six years ago about taxes. The kid hadn't paid any in his whole life. No taxes. Never filed. Not that he made that much money, but . . .

"Is that nuts or what? What was he thinking? Ya gotta pay something. They got people working day and night to find the dummies who don't turn in a tax form."

Cockren goes crazy on him telling him what to do and how to do it. The kid tells him to fuck off and it almost comes to blows. But it doesn't. It just takes on the form of words. Words ya can't take back. Mostly out of Cockren's mouth.

"That's progress. Me at nineteen and that guy they called my father. Oh what a night that was! I let him go to it. The eventual justification for me being a piece of shit the rest of my life. And on that night, the final night, I kept telling him, spitting blood I'm telling him. 'Give it all you got you Popso 'cause when you're done, I'm gonna still be here and you'd better hope that I got more heart in me than you do, fuckhead.'

"Let me tell you something. The brutes, they know when it's over, when their turn's around the corner. They know when to lay off and play another angle, pretend that nothin' happened. They even joke about it like it was a TV episode or something. And they duck the bullet."

"I wanted give him something different
But didn't know how.
I wanted to show him the red leaves
And the fire of autumn;

35

The tall grass and quiet graves.
I wanted to take back the too soon
And the too much and the too hard
And give him something different."

On January 23 of this past year Cockren went to his first heavy metal concert at a beat-up bowling alley on the northwest side. Gothic metal heads wall to wall. Some of them very very large. Inside Cockren was afraid and he hated that. He hated their music. He hated the symbols of power they adorn themselves with. The pulse. The makeup. The dirty looks. The threatening postures. He stood out like the weirdest dude in their dark universe: loafers, powder-blue jeans, a yellow knit shirt with a little alligator emblem on it, and his white well-groomed hair. He was there to see Buck's latest band, Peeled Skin, and for the past three months they'd been talkin'.

"Without drawing no conclusions, just listening. I just listen. He can say whatever he wants to. His freaked-up buddies come in and sit down next to us in the restaurant like it's a drug deal. They say hello Mr. Cockren. I nod. They leave. I make no comment after they're gone. I just smile.

"And here's the thing . . . I ain't gonna make it through this. Only you. I'm telling only you, this goes nowhere. I grew up being told not to be this way and it was wrong. I can see that now but I ain't got that much time to change. But I'm trying, you can see that I'm trying.

"So here's what it is. He's up there in this shithole with these fucked-up kids dressed like the Adamms Family all around sneering at me like vipers. He's up on the stage directing people 'cause he's the only one who knows what he's doing, I can see that. The tech stuff ain't right and he's up there fixin' it when everybody else is chopped-off chicken heads he's . . . my kid . . . he knows what he's doing and then . . .

". . . then he starts to play. He plays this synthetic organ thing, you know, with the buttons and patches, plays any instrument you want only it's electronic. He plays it and . . . he's good . . . real good. Alive. Accomplished. And . . . and I'm looking at him in the black light with the strobes flashing and . . . and I love him. I love him again. I ain't loved this kid for six years, but here I am lovin' him in the middle of this hellhole. And I ain't stopped lovin' him. I've seen him every week for the past six months. Ain't that nuts? In the middle of all this evil shit I'm hating I love him."

This is not too far from the truth for all of us. By the time Cockren finished his story we were both crying. Two old men sobbing in the Golden Nugget surrounded by twenty other broken lives. They've all been there. Al, the Greek cook, comes over and asks if there was something he could do. Cockren hides his face. I start to laugh. What a sight! Old men crying. Nothing more pathetic. Nothing more real.

"Hey pal, you'll be old one day too pal, get ready."

MY FATHER'S COAT

I'm wearing my father's coat.
He has died. I didn't like him,
But I wear the coat.

I'm wearing the coat of my father,
Who is dead. I didn't like him,
But I wear the coat just the same.

A younger man, stopping me on the street,
Has asked,
"Where did you get a coat like that?"

I answer that it was my father's.
Now gone, passed away.
The younger man shuts up.

It's not that I'm trying now
To be proud of my father.
I didn't like him.
He was a narrow man.

There was more of everything he should have done.
More of what he should have tried to understand.

The coat fit him well.
It fits me now.
I didn't love him,
But I wear the coat.

Most of us show off to one another
Fashions of who we are.
Sometimes buttoned to the neck.

Sometimes overpriced.
Sometimes surprising even ourselves
In garments we would have never dreamed of wearing.

I wear my father's coat.
And it seems to me
That this is the way the most of us
Make each other's acquaintance—
In coats we have taken
To be our own.

CORNERS

I'm in the Buckin' A Café in Bucktown payin' a buck and some small change for an offbeat cup of coffee, black. I've just tramped down from Belmont along Damen in an ice storm. It's after Christmas, still December, 1990 something.

The coffee comes over to me cold and thick—bad form in a big big cup. I look at it and think, "Maybe this was once a soup bowl converted now into a condominium for cappuccino, espresso, and mocha locha. How clever."

Clever is a concept I want to scrape out of my brain, a thought storm I caught in the cold, an impulse to write about cornered people intersecting inside and out. Right-angulars perpendicular to everything and everyone else.

The waitress posing as the owner, or is it the owner posing as a waitress? Or is it an actor posing as them both? I can't be sure. Whoever it is crosses the room confidently toward me toeing one of those offbeat, artistic, can't-miss vectors of mainline success, the kind so recently formulated block by block by the lately local gentry who now serve the hood blue-blooded muffins and buttery altruistic words advocating community reemergence.

She stoops at my table and asks, "Is it okay? The coffee? From the bottom of the pot. I'm sorry. It looks terrible. How does it taste? I have some fresh brewing. Would you?"

"No." I reply, "This is fine." And then she smiles. Not an authentic smile. Not even the obligatory I'm-the-waitress-it's-my-job smile. No, this clear-eyed, clean-toothed, heaving heartbeat-on-a-sleeve bares her soul and shapes her face as if to say, "You can tell me anything. I'm here to be your best friend."

Corners start doubling over in my brain, frostbitten wanderers superimposing themselves on everything I see. I want to capture them, these cornered people. The ones I've passed along my way. Freeze them in an ice storm of my own. Not the homeless, but those who know their homes too well. Who pace their blocks like jailbird dogs out for daily exercise. Who mutter and fidget and fumble though their pockets for things they do not own.

But my concentration cannot keep within this cornered zone. It's broken by an intrusive species, by the white wail of "respect" blowing its hole out of a suburban brine, by a McDumpling dumped into my greasy-spoon thoughts, by a cocksure come from money spick-and-span boogalooin' boy-man beating his designer chest in the northwest corner of the Buckin' A.

"Respect! R-E-S-P-E-C-T!" He howls it out as if he were a college quarterback calling signals inside the ten yard line going in for the goal on a keeper's play.

I look up and see him rolling his fists around about in the air doing the monkey, turning the volume up on an antique Zenith radio as he copycats Aretha in a cut up for his friends.

I become depressed. My mind shuts down like a Bucktown factory. Gutted. Going. Gone. Yawning for redevelopment.

The privileged boy, who thinks himself a man because Pappy shines his shoes while Philipo, the barber, shaves his fuzzy face, finishes his antics and adjusts the volume down on the antique Zenith radio. "Thank God."

And just as the fragments of my mind are about to reassemble, I hear him urge his blemish-free friends to go with him tonight and "do" some poetry. "Do" as if he were going to dine on Chinese or sushi.

The gals and the guys bite down on their scones offering up between chews a litany of cafés, clubs, and cabarets where they've heard that people "do" poetry.

The monkey dancer sporting a smirk (as if he knew the scones were stale before he ordered them for his pals) says, "Yeah. Poetry is real trendy now."

"Poetry is real trendy now?" I hear this and begin to boil. "Poetry is real trendy now!" Pigeons fly out of my head. "Poetry is trendy." Hot coals in oil drum barrels begin to glow and pulsate. The control rods are withdrawn. The reactor heats up.

"Poetry is real trendy now!!!!" Somehow I feel responsible, cornered by this comment. I want to get up and kick his wealthy suburban import ass out of this city, out of this neighborhood . . . which isn't my own . . . but I was born and raised in Chicago and I have some rights!

I begin to visualize pouring the vomit of broken lives down his and his friends' orthodontally redecorated gullets. I see myself smearing their complexions with the pea-green soup I supped at the Belmont Café. I want to break their cocksure conquering grip on life and make them feel the everyday pain of everyone else.

But I'm an old man now, increasingly more unsure of myself . . . and I never was that tough anyway. So instead, I discreetly pay my bill, leave a modest tip, and head back up to Belmont, sleet slipping over my shoes, my indigent speech unsaid.

When I arrive back at my bench, I sit down, newspaper under my seat, patting my knees trying to keep my fingers from the cold.

BREAKFAST

I gotta get me to breakfast
Down at the greasy spoon.
Order up some hash browns,
Over-easies, bacon too.
Need a 4 a.m. breakfast!
Pork patties and a heap o' cakes.
Pick up tomorrow's news.
Read a line and gobble up

A poached-egg politician cuts off
Corned beef fine arts from the poor
French toast meter on Cabbie out
Comin' in quick stop oatmeal
Cream o' Wheat, Belgian waffles,
Denver omelet, cheese blintzes . . .
Baby, I need more jelly.

Cook me up some breakfast,
Fast-order Paper Hat!
He grumbles out a bad joke.
Half the counter laughs at it.
It's a 4 a.m. breakfast.
Night birds down to roost.
Haunches on the chrome stools
Spooning up

Biscuits, gravy, BO, bad breath,
Wigs fallin' off, strawberry crepes,
Scrambled pig's feet in a jar,
American morning fried specials,
Skirt steaks, hash . . . "Hashimoto!
Someone's swiping your bass
Out of the back seat of your car!"

OJ   TJ   BJ
Where's that jelly?

I need a hot-buttered breakfast.
My chops are a bowl o' mush.
Sweetheart, I'm fallin' out.
My tongue's tired, very soft.
Could we please break for . . .
You know you'd like to kill this man.
Honey, Baby, I'm gonna need some sustenance
If we're going to carry on like this.

Just get me to breakfast!
I don't care where I go
Got to fill my belly with

> *Carbohydrate globs!*
> *Pigs in a blanket, 4 deuces,*
> *Grits, Danish, donuts,*
> *A slice of grilled ham.*

> *Kellogg's Corn Flakes!*
> *Bring me some cream.*
> *How much is that cheesecake?*
> *I'll take two pieces of pie*
> *And a breakfast burrito.*
> *How do you say this,*
> *Chiney Cahtas—Number 8?*
> *Early bird silver dollar slider special.*
> > *Coffee?*
> *You're askin' Marc Smith*
> *If he wants more coffee?*
> *Of course he does.*

And get him to breakfast.
He don't care where he goes.
Gotta get some breakfast
Before it dawns . . . before it dawns . . . before it dawns . . .

STUTTERING LIGHT

There was a sixteen-millimeter emotion machine
Propped up on books in the back of his head
Projecting love onto his late-night street-wandering teens
Lacing them with music, corny music,
Music that seemed to color each raindrop silver.
Bouncing rhapsodies of raindrops silver.
Bouncing off springboard avenues.
Sparkling stuntman leaps
Into the streetlamp light
Down through which he wandered
Trailing the lonely haunting calls of
　　　Could be? Who knows?

I guess he was trapped by that.
By the splash and curl and draw
Of the ocean over a beach
Where he and his love would fall spinning,
Slowly spinning arms entangled
Down to where the water would wet their skin
Warm and colored by the rose-red setting sun.
Silhouettes backed by a paramount horizon.
That kind of emotion was pictured in his love
Laced with corny music.
Enchanting, entrapping music.
Music he'd be the first to tell you now
Was ever in his head.
It came from the movies.
From the close-up kisses.
From the intent expressions of
What else could make the world so right?

His love gripping the arms of the one
He thought he'd hold forever.
Pulling her upward to his descending kiss.
Telling her everything about all there was of him.
Placing his trust perpendicular to the image
He wanted most truly always ever to be his own.

It came from the movies.
The clothed embrace.
The tears welling up.
The violins.
Old movies.
Love without an afterward.
Without explicit definition.
Without technique.

I guess he was trapped by that.
It made a music sing inside his head.
It threw aside reason
And eventually

              it snapped

    And went flapping
    Around and around
    On the reel.

White light.
White screen.
It came from the movies.

THE RUSH STREET SHUFFLE

Free shots! . . . . *Free shots!*

           Freeeeeeeeeeeeeeeeeeeeeeeeeeee

SHOTS!   *FREESHOTS!*

Two for one watermelons! No cover. No min (imum).
        Turn in, good buddy, try our
Fried chicken little legs in a pot of hot sauce,
        Celery, breadsticks, meatballs
On the street: blue ties, green ties, phat thighs.
        Two dollars at the bar.
           C'mon
Upstairs downstairs. Downstairs upstairs.

        We got:
White boy from the burbs, from a dairy farm town.
        East coast. West coast.
        Shoppers off the gold coast.
Low down cross-legged, both arms amputated.
        Black man steppin' out gonna find a white chick.
Educated Serbian, liberated, wants an
        Upper stratum, clean-cut, six-figure Polack.
Move along.
Move along.   Move along.

        We got:
Steroid baby-face, thin-fingered bruisable
        Bouncers bulging out biceps
           Pokin' at
Middleweight, lightweight, wannabe contenders
Move along.
Move along.   Move along the

Blue horse barricade blockin' off the jaywalk.
    Jacksons takin' in
            Comin' out Abrahams.
Jacksons takin' in
            Comin' out Abrahams!
    How about a head wash honey?

        We got:
Puerto Rican cokehead coppin' from a premed.
    Flag wavin' Christians!
            Flag wavin' Christians!
Short skirts. High ass. Short skirts. High ass.
    Waggin' where the dicks pass.
    Waggin' where the dicks pass.

    How about a head wash honey?

        We got:
Overfed unweds hopin' for a hot bed.
Separated middlemen. Can't decide what to do.
Two timin'   three timin'   four timin' hooks

    How about a head wash honey?
    How about that head wash honey?

Free shots! . . . . Free shots!

        Freeeeeeeeeeeeeeeeeeeeeeeeeee

SHOTS!   *FREESHOTS!*

"Okay, right there! There's a spot right there! Do a Bat Turn! Now! Now! Jesus Christ! You-dumb-fuck! You missed it. I ain't payin' no five bucks to park in the lot!"

"Oooooooo wheeeeeeeeeeee mama mama mama come here and sit on my face."

"If this guy is gonna be strokin' his monkey all night long, I want outta this car."

48

"Okay okay! There's another spot. Do a bat turn. TURN AROUND NOW!
I told you I ain't payin' no five bucks to park in the lot!"

Good evening, and excuse me sir, but, in the recent uprisings in the
former Soviet city of Baku, my paternal grandmother—eighty-six years
old–was brutally beaten to death by Islamic zealots. I'm wondering if
you have the charity to spare a few coins so that I might erect a monu-
ment to her in the Graceland Cemetery . . . Oh certainly, I understand.
And blessings to you throughout your busy day.

My my my! Don't we look debonair tonight! And the Mrs.! Quite ele-
gant. Off to the theater? By the by, old boy, might you be able to . . .
Say Bubb! We all gotta make a living! Money don't grow on trees. I
hope you got first row tickets and the Fat Lady lands in your lap!

> Help a veteran get some soup.
> Bums are the snails of the city.

Look Lady, do you think I wanna be out here? Do you think I gotta choice huh
Lady? Do ya? Let me tell you something! Let me tell you something, Lady! I
ain't got no kidneys. That's right. No kidneys. So how am I supposed to go find
work with no kidneys? Huh? Can you tell me that? And you know what else,
Lady? You know what else? If I don't get to a dialysis center pretty quick, pretty
quick, Lady, you know what's gonna happen? I'm gonna urinate in my pants
and all over the street. That's right, Lady. And all these pretty people passing
by are gonna be lookin' at me like I'm some kind of disgusting animal. Do you
want that to happen to me, do ya Lady? Do ya?

> Five dollars? That's it? You spend more than this on nail polish.
> Okay okay. Sure, Lady, when you get back, right.
> Yeah, Lady. I can hold it. Thanks for the concern.

> Bums are the snails of the city.
> Help a veteran get some soup.

Free shots! . . . . Free shots!

Freeeeeeeeeeeeeeeeeeeeeeeeeeeeee

SHOTS!   *FREESHOTS!*

Sinners!
  I hear your words of mockery.
  I see your faces of scorn.
  The Lord hears you.
  The Lord sees you.

The Lord has followed you into
  The Hang-ups!
  The Hangouts!
  The Back Room Snuggeries

He knows what you're thinking.
He knows what's on your minds.
  Fornication!
  Gluttony!
  Avarice!
  Debauchery!

He hears you asking yourselves,
Who is this soul standing out in the cold
Confronting us and calling us

  Sinners!

What does this holy man in the tan trench coat
Know of the ways of
  Our World!
By what right does he
With his Bibled hands
And black buckled boots
Confront us and call us

  Sinners!

Well,
  Sinners!
I know who you are.
I know your iniquities.

I am not a hypocrite.
I have sinned.
I am sinful.

I have masturbated into the pages of dirt magazines.
I have attended the peep shows and stayed for hours.
I have taken the harlot and plugged his behind.

But

    Sinners!

The Lord is with me now!
I know Him.

    Sweet Glory be mine forever!

No longer do I have lust in my heart!
No longer do I have pride!
No longer envy!
No longer do I feed my face
Dunkin' Donuts
At 2 a.m. like a swine!

No! Sweet Glory Be Mine Forever!

Now I stand on this street corner night after night
Preaching to people who ignore me, despise me,
Spit on me, flip me the bird.

And I say to you: What could be better?
What could be better than to know that the Sweet Gates of Glory
Will be open to me at my appointed hour?
WHAT COULD BE BETTER!

Free shots! . . . . *Free shots!*

    Freeeeeeeeeeeeeeeeeeeeeeeeeeee

SHOTS!

ROSIE

This is how it lays out.
I'm off work pushing it.
Had to do the overtime thing.
Drive a little minivan
Up and down the Gold Coast.
Packages for important people.
Most of whom had it between their lips
All their lives.
The silver spoon that is.
Socially liberal, but fiscally
They know how to hold on to it real tight.
Ski the last chance slopes of spring.
Sail the last chance flutters of autumn.
Ride their hot fanny panties
Up and down on carousel horses
Copped from the World's Fair
Right there in own living rooms
Underneath the antique gas lamps.

It's a priority delivery service.
To work it you gotta be alert, trim,
Play the lower-caste type.
Feet-on-the-bootstrap attitude.
They like that.
Helps to be as brown as they are,
But not from the sun—
Born that way.
Schmooz 'em with the fierce hard look
Of your stone-black eyes
Followed by a twisted grin,
Followed by the prattle of a comeback tongue.
Guilt-trip sarcasm. Works every time.

They like the smell and taste of a fight
As long as they can close the door on it,

Anyway, I made my last drop on Aster Street.
A big-time Art fart. Gave me a twenty-buck tip.
Pink eyes. Puffy lids. Had the sniffles.
You get the picture.

Thank you, sir, I say grabbing the cash
Hoppin' down the brownstone stairs.
In two hoots I'm back in the van
Turning the throttle up on Clark Street
Heading south for cocktail heaven.
I was late and I didn't want to be.
Had a date with one fine lady.
Didn't want to miss a chance like that.
But then this long lurching limo
Pulls out in front of me real slow
Like it didn't give a shit
Like it was the only cocksucker left in the world.
"Hey bug face! Get your steel ass out of the way!"

The back black window rolls down automatic
And a thin pale female hand drops out a cigarette.
As I pass by ready to finger the face inside
I see the eyebrow pencil glare staring into nowhere
And it hits me, "That's Rosie!
Rosie from the old neighborhood.
What's she doin' in there?"

There's a silver-bullet lining and an olive in her throat
And a ring the size of Jupiter
On a finger she taps on the mahogany rail.
Her long pink painted nails scratch the cellophane wrap
As the man stooling next to her
Leans uprightly forward to light her smoke.

She's the girl of his dreams,
The one he's always calling for
To come in a late-night negligee
To smooth his trembling skin
Until he cries out,
"Baby baby baby
Like a rattle shake it, baby,
C'mon, baby, shake it."

She's the girl of his dreams.
And as the moonlight through the window falls upon her face
The branches of the hucklebuck cast dark impressions
Of thornlike fingers
That poke her places she doesn't want him to see
"Don't see!" or touch "Don't touch" the blue vein,
The mark behind her contorted knee,
The scar running lengthwise head to toe.

She's the girl of his dreams
And as he stomachs her around
Pressing her shoulders to the sheet
On the flip side her heart
His hairy knuckles arched her upward like a cat
Like a cat swimming up from a bag in the river
To pillows of silk and candlelight perfume
And the music she keeps to herself
As he fondles hypnotically
The rhythmic sway of her ass.

She's the girl of his dreams,
The one fanning limousines,
The painted Mother Mary sister someone
Seen like a white flower on a black bow
Along Chestnut sky-high avenues.
Rosie! The goddess! The vision she lets out,
Makes out, throws off the curl of her lips
To turn him upstanding cream
Snorting out his kind of love,

"Baby baby baby" until he's done "Baby baby baby"
And he wheezes out the other end "baby baby baby."

Finished, she stands in the shadows by her dresser in the dark
Over a candle where she shoots and sings,
"This is the boy of my dreams.
The pretty powder god I'm always waiting for."

"Hey, that's Rosie! Rosie from the old neighborhood.
What's she doin' in there?"

MOON MOAN

There was a moan in his memory. Dust floating up from his dying mother's mouth. Off notes plopping kerplunk into a crater. Sound waves echoing back upon him pressing hard against the taut fabric of his tightened mind as he fell asleep wondering what mallet had struck him and what the moon moans meant.

Was it "no no no" or "oh" or just the muffled drone of bedded voices bouncing slowly in a moonlit room? Was it a man-made shadow standing at the doorway clutching moonbeams beating his mother? Were they making moonbeam love? Did they enter his room? Did she save him? The moan . . . was it real at all?

When he sat down to dinner watching his mother consume packaged cookies, crumbling each one into the reboiled coffee of last night's late TV, he wished he could ask her about the moan and all the cryptic things left moon stuck in his memory like a complicated radio apparatus transmitting untranslatable messages from deep intangible space.

Her face, a landscape of lunar rock crossed by arid river canyons, had a yellowing tone. He squinted to see if any water whatsoever flowed out and down along her caved-in cheeks.

"No" or "Oh" she only asked about the weather dabbing arthritic fingers at the curbs around her cup to capture lost particles and lift them off the Formica into her soundless mouth.

Once he almost dared his lips to break the spell and push them pell-mell into the hollow gravity of her haunted core. But the steles of her stony eyes lifted, signs of trespass forbidden, and he shriveled, tongue dry, as silent as the surface of the moon.

IMPUDENCE

Excuse me, you dropped something.

I was passing their booth
Crowded with casual arms and laughter
Next to the foyer. I was
Coming in from the street noise,
Rain on my shoulders,
An old man seeking a bowl of soup,
Crackers, and coffee.

Excuse me, you dropped something.

What? Dropped something?
I looked down. I knew I hadn't—
Instinct's way of knowing the truth
Even if your consciousness is foggy.
I looked down, behind, to the side,
Wondering,
What did Youth see that I didn't?
The booth of them
Stone-faced for a moment watching me.

Oh I guess you didn't.

Prompting a communal guffaw
Followed by muffled snickers.
Guffaw, snicker, yuck yuck yuck.
Oh, a joke! A joke on the old man!
Selfie entertainment.
This is how Youth passes empty afternoons,
Preying on the feebleminded
From fake-leather seats in a transient café.

Oh I guess you didn't.

And it was the straight-faced impudence
That got the old goat. The deadpan eyes.
The contempt behind the mask, the prejudice.

Oh I guess you didn't. Snicker snicker snicker.

"Excuse me," I wanted to rejoin,
My own play on Youth's idle effrontery.
"Excuse me, but your nose ring isn't rad.
And your hair, moussed and tinted, isn't shocking.
Your black lipstick made to match your manicured claws
Is not the Devil's mark. It's bad fashion.

"Excuse me,
But you are the most affluent generation of rebels
I've ever been snickered by.
What are you revolting against?
The dysfunction of your cell phone?
The tragedy of your misplaced iPod?

"Excuse me, but
Why are you bumming for change?
Why are you tricking for kicks?
Why are you pretending to be ghetto?
Can't you find something less overdone to do?

"Pardon me, but
The world's collapsing on your watch.
Time to kneel down and count the dead.
Time to face the fire hose.
Time to wrestle the K-9s on *your* block.

"Excuse me, but
Why don't you cross your own color?
Challenge your own dumb thoughts?
Question the smug mug in the mirror?
Why don't you . . . ?"

And then the group gaggled heigh-ho!
Guffaw, snicker, yuck yuck yuck.
Goosefleshing the heat on my grumpy face
As I squared and turned toward the counter
Taking my position on a stool
Hunkering down to sup my soup alone.

ARNOLD THE JAZZ PROPHET

Arnold enters with his ax and blows.

That was a poem. A tone poem.

Blows a few notes . . . rhymes with *. . . and a few more.*

If you want to play nice you make it rhyme. *(Blows melodic.)* Pretty, eh? Pretty boring! If you don't give a damn! *(Blows hard.)* If nice just ain't where you're at? *(Blows harder.)* If everything that might have been nice for you turned out to be a hacked-up melody on a worn-out riff, then you might be buzzin' your lips on somethin' like this:

Blows hard and wild, then lightens up.

Whichever, whatever the case may be, it is essential for you to blow your soul. Blow your goddamned soul. Take your tired ass out to the water's edge, stand your feet upon a stony pier, look down into that frothy white foam, and blow all there is into that blue-green spray.

It's puking up color, man! Throwin' it up. Throwin' it down. Throwin' it up. Throwin' it down. It's the universal Jacuzzi, Jackson! Every bit of everything there ever was in a hocker of spit!

I'm tellin' ya, you've got to blow every goddamned note you ever heard off the hooks inside your head. Evacuate the torment, man. Don't let it cramp you up. Clear the room! Evacuate! Expand the nucleus!

Blows wild again.

The landlord upstairs! He is a tyrant! Money and time are all he cares about. He's working on a deadline. He wants to put you on that deadline. He wants to string you out on a long cord and knot your progress. And ooouuuu weeee!

when he ties those knots the rope whips 'round and 'bout and you don't know who the fuck you are until he stretches you out on it again.

The landlord upstairs is a very uncool dude. Don't let him tie you up. Time ain't his to appropriate. Time ain't nothin'! Let me show you what you can do to Time!

Blows but freezes in a soundless pose for several seconds.

It's your soul, man, the blue-green wave. You've been throwin' all your shit into it. It looks like the landlord's tabletop piled up with perpetual paperwork. Clear it off! Make some room! Clean the wave. Blow it cool. Blow it dreamy. But blow your soul, man. Blow your goddamned soul.

TURNING TEN

During fifth grade library period, Davy Luper lifted his nose over his book to admire Andy Spur's eyes registering volumes of lines left to right, left to right, down the page, zip zip zip! Now *there* was a boy who could read. And Davy was fascinated by and envious of Andy's eyes, which every now and then would push themselves bulging out of their sockets like William F. Buckley Jr.'s yawning and stretching wide awake in the red, white, and blue American atmosphere.

Firing line fast those pupils would bull's-eye the p's and q's, ingest the ideologies, snap the covers shut, and flip the spines back on the shelves filing down the rows hup hup hup in search of another. All before Davy could even figure out what the first word on the third line of the first page of the book he was pretending to read was.

And then, strutting proud, as if on post parade, Andy's fingers would march along the Dewey Decimal digits inspecting the labels in search of a next new title to conquer, revved up like a motorcade MP patrolling foreign soil brashly sending a siren scream into the dead night air calling for "More Words! More Words!"

All this before Davy had been able to set his sights upon deciphering the descriptive captions under the Marine Corps Action Photos in the picture books he stuck his nose in during third-period library session examining and analyzing the photographic deeds done by realistic service daddies on duty in Japan throwing bloated Hiroshima bodies onto the back beds of dump trucks for sacred mass burials.

But, of course, those pictures were not included in the books Davy and Andy were given to read. Their books showed Sergeant John Wayne defending his country, flag, and everybody's smiling grandmother—not to mention their right to even be there on their soft behinds in stateside schoolhouse libraries reading pages of picture-book history.

And while Davy wasted semesters away daydreaming of flushing out a fearsome enemy with a flamethrower on a peninsula somewhere in the South Seas, Andy Spur's eyes marched double time toward an educated Nam-sized second looie package of grief opened up—surprise!—on a hillside somewhere north of Sector C becoming the gloriously unsung hero Davy had wished himself to be someday when he was West Point well read as Andy.

And after all those books conspicuously consumed in the fifth grade, Andy Spur came home to his mother wrapped in plastic, pieces of his fast brain popped out of his skull like those bulging eyes Davy so much admired.

SMALL TALK

Sure hope it don't rain today.
Weatherman's calling for 30 percent chance.

> Hey, ya can't trust what a weatherman says.
> He ain't no meteoragist. He's an actor.

Not even actor. A quack!
Scientologist, he is not.

Maybe we're in for a drought.

> A drought?

Yeah.

> That's cuz the jet stream got shifted around.

By a volcano.

> Not just one volcano, a whole string of volcanoes.
> All over the world. Sunspots, too.

Actually, it might be . . .

The ozone!
Moisture goes up through the hole,
Evaporates into space, dampens the sun.

Naw. Naw. Naw. That would make it cold.
What really happened is . . .

> They screwed up the water table.
> Cracked it.

Steam comes up from the core,
Goes through the crack,
Dries up everything.

Well, whatever it is,
We're in for a drought.
Does that make you happy?

Happy?

Hey, the way I heard it,
It's some kinda nuclear thing.
Out west in Colorado.

Not Colorado. Not even the U. S. of A.
It's Korea.

Naw. Naw. That's what they want you to think.
The one to watch is China.

Wrong again.
Not Colorado. Not China. Not Korea.
But it's out west, all right.
California.
California produce farmers are sucking up all the water
To make fruit grow where it ain't supposed to.
You can look it up on the internet.
It's a matter of public record.

If you'd just take a couple minutes
To step back and get some perspection,
You'd see that the whole problem is
Speculators, plain and simple.
Always has been, always will be.
They gobble up everything to make a quick buck.
Started in on the rain decades ago.
Next they'll go after the sun.
Hell, they probably already have.

You got any idea how many solar panels
In this state alone? Think on that!
And then think about Arizona.

Arizona?

Wrong again.
It ain't speculators.
It ain't sunspots.
It ain't Arizona.

It's the Militiamen.
Survivalists are hoardin' the water
In plastic milk jugs
Waiting for doomsday.
Part one of their twofold plan—
Hoard the water
And harass the liberals.
Start a revolution,
Blame it on the government,
And when the bullets fly,
Who's got the guns?

Jesus Christ,
If ya'd read the newspapers now and then
Maybe ya'd get the big picture.
Race. It's all a matter of race.
Right there in black and white.
Scientists discovered a time sucker
At the edge of the Milky Way.
We're zoomin' toward it
In one big cosmic race.
Interstellar confrontation.
Positive and negative protons,
X & Y factors infesting the neutrinos
Pow! Pow! Pow!

Makes all your earthbound babble
Seem pretty silly, don't it?
Trouble with you guys is
You never take a look at the nighttime sky.
You're always nose deep in the dirt
Waiting for a geyser to shoot up
And knock your head off.

A geyser?

Well, I just thought . . .

A drought?

Tomorrow?

Fat chance.

AMERITECH

The phone rings and I move to answer it. My ear is hot. Not more than a few minutes ago another ring rang the bell for the fourth time on this Sunday afternoon rehearsing for the big show tonight that I want to do so well in.

Why am I answering it? Haven't I had enough local/long-distance jabs for one day? Mrs. Ex's explicit explanations of why I am certainly still a jerk for having only signed over all the accounts and half the house to her. Shouldn't I also be supplementing her approaching-six-digit annual income with a percentage of my princely poet's pot of gold? After all, I am the Man and the father of her children.

No. I should let the phone ring. The machine will handle it. NO! Why is my hand reaching toward it automatically as if demonically possessed, ready to be instantly candid, honest to the point of agony, preprogrammed to be forever Lutheran, to set my head upon the chopping block. Be it friend or flotsam I will answer each and every inquisition without a mere moment's hesitation.

"Hello."
"Mr. Smith?"
"Yes."
"Mr. Smith, I'm Jean Jane Joan of the Megatropolis Midtown Communications Complex. We're compiling information for a story to be aired on our Print Tube Tape Tabloid Internet Network. We'd like to interview you concerning your *involvement* with the Poetry Slam. Have you a few minutes to spare?"

There! There is where you should say no. Hang up quickly.

"Well, yeah, I guess so."

WHY!?! WHY did you say YES?!? You've told yourself a trillion times, no more interviews. You're gonna suck hard again, Marc.

"Well, yeah, I guess so."

"Great! Let's get started then. Mr. Smith, when did you first come in contact with the Poetry Slam?"

"Uh . . . well . . . I started it."

"You started the poetry slams of Chicago? When was that?"

"Uh . . . 1986. July 1986, but things really began at a little place called . . ."

"What motivated you to start your slam? Were you influenced by the Nuyorican Poets of New York? Or did Henry Rollins give you the spark that inspired you? We've heard you've taken his style and made it your own."

"UH . . . you see . . . uh . . . I think . . . uh . . . I might have had . . . a little . . . influence . . . on . . ."

Hold back, Marc. Don't lose it. Don't start whining again. This is America. Nobody gives a shit where stuff comes from. You didn't care who the current poet gods and goddesses were when you came stomping through the garden laughing at the Apple. It's your karma catching up with you, Marc. Hold back!

"Look, honey, didn't you do any research before you called. The slam . . ."

Down the block, across the street, Manny, my Mexican neighbor, is corralling his two-year-old granddaughter, who tumbles and rises learning to walk. Manny has what I want, an aged and loving heart. He sweetly guides what's grown from him.

An hour ago on the phone my son and I volleyed words harsh and bitter. My mind aches with the thought that I am losing him.

Now, this careless reporter on a deadline with success snips unknowingly the straps wrapped round my bruised and swelling core. She does not know, nor does she care to know, that below the surface of the wound she opens, beyond the fifteen minutes her interview will play, apart from the "get ahead" hum of the airways, outside the circles of lights, action, camera

> There are families reeling in chaos.
> There are children recklessly alone.
> There are people embattled and bitter.

And there is this constant, alluring Capital ring . . . ring . . . ring . . . fame and fortune calling . . .

> Marc! Marc! Please! . . . Don't answer.

DEEP-DISH CHICAGO

Written for Chicago's Stirring Things Up Festival

Chicago: the deep-dish city of deep-dish people
    Everybody's juices bubblin' & sizzlin' & spittin' inside.

        And a crust that can be thick, when it needs to be thick
        When it gets poked and fingered and belittled;
        Cast off as just another second-city helping—
            Flatlander windy cheese.

But we know better. We who live in this city and love its people
    know that it's SECOND TO NONE when it comes to a slice
        Of authenticity, genuine, no BS . . . "Skip the pretense, pal."
                                "Hey, you ain't puttin' that
                                pomposity
        Second to none when it comes   *into my pizza pie, amigo!"*
        To feeding a vision of *yes* to no small dreams
        Of can do. Go for it. Make it happen.

And then,
        Stand back and watch the world beyond our crust
        Try to lay claim to the juices we cooked up,
        That we brought to life. That we passed on as a gift of nutrition
        To those who have hungered for a spirit like ours.

So here's duh scoop: This deep dish of *do it* comes from us,
        From our city and our people . . .
                "Hey Lou, tell the poet, 'Enough talk,
            let's eat!'"

*There are a couple of good stories that go along with this poem. It debuted at a press con-
ference for the 2003 Stirring Things Up Festival. The Speak'Easy Ensemble provided backup
vocals to my front man performance as they emerged from behind the audience accenting and

echoing sections of the poem, and causing a little stir among the dignitaries, politicians, and reporters not used to slam anarchy or in-audience poetic presentations.

On the last lines, however, some of those same stone-faced politicians were teary-eyed with civic pride and sentimentality . . . and when a stack of Lou Malnati's pizzas arrived on the cue of "Let's eat!" a little roar of pleasure went up as they all hurried to devour the deep-dish reality.

Following the ceremony and throughout the summer copies of the poem were delivered to a few thousand people inside Lou Malnati pizza boxes. Not one person ever told me that they noticed the poem—not even my son, who ordered pizzas from Malnati's on a regular basis. Proof positive that pizza takes precedence over poems where Chicago's appetites are concerned.

It ain't something you can purchase.
You ain't gonna find *it*
At the Merchandise Mart.

It ain't a brain thing.
It can't be calculated.
You can read about *it*
In a book,
But *it* ain't there.

Maybe at one time
You thought you saw *it*
In the silver glaze
Of an old theatrical photograph
Framed in the family album

Or heard it off a Blue Note label
Sounding a feathery sequence
Of "Moonlight Serenade."

Or sensed it in the clacking keys
Of a beat-up saxophone
Compelling you to listen.

But by now
Those things are once
Twice . . . three times removed,
Pawned to some old man in a hockshop
Cluttered up with all the things of value
We traded in for a spell.
To make ends meet, we said.
But weren't we really saying that

That's to be the end of *it*?
That it's all to be left
Hanging on a hook,
Tarnished in a velvet case,
Mute behind a glass door,
Sleeping in a box?

The end of *it*
Inside of us for sure,
Where it refrains every day
When we can't drag ourselves up out of bed.
Every night
When we can't keep our eyelids from dropping down
Like the hockshop's roll-up shutter door
Padlocked at the bottom.

Don't we hear the groaning ghost of *it*
In the machines we drive to work each day?
In the etiquette and protocol
Of our office-building pals?

In the clocks!
Oh don't we definitely hear
The groaning ghost of *it*
In the clocks?

Or see it in the faces?
In the millions of faces
Marching dull eyed down Michigan,
Shopping on State Street,
Banking in Berwyn?

Or *it's* there all right!
The groaning ghost of *it* is there,
But the live flesh and blood *it* ain't.

If someone outside the Water Tower Place
Or under Picasso's dog

Were to take out that tarnished
Upside-down question mark,
Lick the reed on just what had to be said,
Blow out to all the passing heads:

Listen to me! Listen to me!
I have found IT! I have found IT!

Wouldn't the most of us
Just sidestep a circle around that cat?
Maybe toss a few quarters at his case?
Turn our heads straight forward,
Resume the march
Foot ahead of frantic foot
Trying to distance ourselves from that music,
Trying to keep it out of our hearts,
Trying not to wonder,
What was our ticket number?
    Where is that pawn shop door?

If you need to kiss it,
Kiss it.
If you need to kick it,
Kick it.
If you need to scream it,
Scream it.

But kiss it, kick it, scream it
Now.

If you need to leave it,
Leave it.
If you need to love it,
Love it.
If you need to hold it,
Hold it.

But leave it, love it, hold it
Now.

If you need to squeeze it,
Squeeze it.
If you need to spill it,
Spill it.
If you need to tell the world
You've got more to you
Than the world has as of yet
Allowed you to be,

Then
Be it! Tell it! Spill it!
Squeeze it out of each instantaneous moment.
Make the juice, the jive, the jazz, the jism,
The mysticism that ism you!

Grab at the moon!
And hold the stars hot inside your head.

'Cause now is all there ever was
And all there ever will be.

So kiss it, kick it, scream it
Now!

SOMETHING

There is something of something around us,
Within us, between us.

A something of something heard sometimes
In the sound of one instrument at play.

There is brilliance and death in each note
That vibrates off the string into the wind,
Into the breath of the wind
Like a sigh that precipitates upon our perceptions
    Unnamed, unsolved resolution—
    Resolution building like white cumulonimbus clouds
    Above city skyline stone and steel,
    Above platforms and pedestrians, stone walks and fountains,
    Above pigeons and passers-by to be.

Building more mysteriously
Than the unseen pressure of air
That builds over idle sunporch afternoons
Where idle manuscripts,
    Blank and silent so long,
    Are suddenly overturned
    By new accords of weather sounding with every breath,
    New rattlings, new taps of the branch against the window,
    New scratchings at the door begging to be brought in.

There is something in the wind, in the music, in the loneliness
That carries us back to the beginning
To the cloud's face, to the yellow jacket's churr,
To the parting and the convergence,
To the dark red rapture within the bone's marrow.

And whatever that something is
Contained in the wind, in the music, in the loneliness,
It strains against its boundaries
To be found, to be free,
To be resolute in the storm bent bending of stems,
     In the beating rapture of rain,
     In the vibrations of the strings set to motion
     By fingers commanding allegiance
     From each of the keys as they are played
     By that something of something around us
          Between us   Within.